Praise for **"Crimson Stain"**

"I first became aware of Dee Allen's work a year prior to the COVID Pandemic when he read at Sacred Grounds Café in San Francisco. To say he made a lasting impression is an understatement. His distinct enunciation along with his poetic and historical social ills marked him as an artist to take seriously. Since then, I've heard Dee read his work several times via Zoom and I've read a number of his previous books. He never falters, never disappoints. With his latest, 'Crimson Stain', Dee Allen continues to elevate his searing poetic indictments against racism, gentrification, sexism, capitalism and militarism, among other cancers on our collective health. But that's not all. With aching sensitivity, more than a few poems fearlessly examine loneliness. And in 'Offering', he has created an erotic poem both boldly personal and transcendent. This collection is nothing short of astounding."

—**Robert Eugene Rubino**, author of the poetry collections *Vanity Unfair* and *Douglas KOs Tyson*

"Dee Allen's newest poetry collection *CRIMSON STAIN: POEMS INSPIRED BY KING'S LETTER FROM JAIL, REAL LIFE AND A FACET OF BLOOD DIAMOND CULTURE* is an enjoyable read from start to finish. From the beginning poem *Loyal To None* to the ending poem *Flamethrower*, every one of these poems will have every reader hooked. Get ready to laugh, to cry and feel various other emotions while reading this phenomenal collection of stellar poetry inspired by the late, great Dr. Martin Luther King, Jr."

—**Olusheyi Banjo** [Big O.], poet and host of the variety podcast *Big O's Top 20 Countdown*

"Reading Dee Allen's current collection draws you in like a serial drama be streamed as a box set. After each poem I wanted to read the next one. Each literal creation increases in its intensity and passion. A collection that can be read repeatedly. Dee has the insight of a prophet and as an activist of good. Dee's poetry is captivating and lives in the truth that is rarely seen now."

—**Gary Huskisson**, storyteller and poet, director of Stroud Against Racism, activist at Say It Louder – Petersborough U.K.

"Dee Allen takes his readers on a voyage into the deepest, darkest things people despise hearing—the visceral truth, that is, life in America as a Black man is more than M & W's definition of struggle. War is Hell. At times explosive, these poems open your senses to sights and sounds , cultivated by centuries of dedicated freedom writers, and manifest as stories from the neverending saga. From capitalism and racism, symbolism to religion, these pages scream for equality, autonomy and true justice. Another masterful work of art from a dedicated creative, armed with the power, to say what he means and mean what he says."

—**Elemen2al**, poet, host of *Nuyorican Poets Café Monday Night Open Mic*, author of *Calamity* [Read Or Green Books], CEO of Elemen2al Visionworx

"Revolutionary artivist Dee Allen searing poetry collection is a poignant reminder to **never** stop questioning the systems that oppress; our survival depends on their unravelment. Allen, himself, is a Flamethrower—casting volcanic infernos of healing towards each injustice he has challenged in a lifetime of activism. His magmatic poetry doesn't burn all down, but, conjures a spark of hope to keep us warm in the quiet moments between battles; a testament to the importance of rest and re-charging while fighting in global movements.

Allen's words are weapons and medicine all at once; a true alchemy of the myriad of discriminations he has dedicated his life to transcending. *Crimson Stain* is a jewel, an ethically-mined jewel, cradled in the hands of our ancestors, rising to reflect the light in this eternal fight for equality and peace in a healing world."

—**Kyla Tucaya Garcia**, actor, director, poet, union member SAG/AFTRA AEA LA/NYC/MT

"Searing poems, a mind questing, navigating amongst the flotsam and jetsam of urban existence, capitalism, wars, the slave trade, death, sweat, sex, proclamations and ripostes—Dee Allen's collection is in dialogue with history, with current justice and injustice, with other writers and thinkers, taking as its keystone King's 'Letter From Birmingham Jail'. Here are lyrics that lay wounds bare, songs of passionate tenderness, verses with the force of slogans, driven throughout by a conviction of our fundamental common humanity."

—**Dr. Amina Alya**l, poet, host of the online open mic *Wordspace*, senior lecturer and programme leader for English & Creative Writing at Leeds Trinity University—Leeds, U.K.

"Dee Allen's *Crimson Stain* should be required reading for all my fellow old white men. We need to be shaken from our comfortable delusion that we live in the Land of the Free. I first became a fan of Mr. Allen during the pandemic when he'd perform at online open mics and I wondered how his work would translate from 'the stage' to 'the page'. I can attest that his charisma carries over, a clarion voice for justice, and his poetry may be even better when read with the eyes where we can better savor the nuance of his language."

—**Bartholomew Barker**, poet, organizer at Living Poetry—North Carolina

"Dee Allen's poems travel the unrealized promises of our American psyche with a restless, unsatisfied yet preserving and balanced voice. Fully rounded poems of protest, celebrations of vibrant spirit, poignant reflection and always a standing up and speaking out, in the tradition of its inspiration, Dr. Martin Luther King Jr's renowned *Letter From Birmingham Jail*. Allen's *Crimson Stain* leads the reader on a devoted sojourn through our highly conflicted present, deeply informed by, as King wrote, *the inescapable network of our mutuality*. In *Crimson Stain*, you will find our humanity overcoming unreason and heartlessness with strength and sensitivity. Dee Allen's words are a balm of steadfastness and balance, he writes poetry infused with conviction and grace."

—**Paul Skiff**, poet, co-producer and creator of sound design for the Nuyorican Symphony

Crimson Stain

POEMS INSPIRED BY KING'S *LETTER
FROM JAIL*,
REAL LIFE AND A FACET OF BLOOD
DIAMOND CULTURE

by

Dee Allen.

PUBLISH

EYEPUBLISHEWE
PUBLISHING POETRY, LITERATURE, ART, MUSIC
FOR HUMANITY'S SAKE
A BRAND NEW PUBLISHING COMPANY
SAN FRANCISCO
FOUNDED 2020

For
John Biocic,
who convinced me to
keep the ink flowing &
to keep the poetry going—

Table of Contents

FOREWORD

Dee Allen is the consummate writer: articulate and eloquent on paper as he is in speech, with an instinctive ability for detail and an ardent cry-out against injustices of any kind. He also shares a passionate love for ecology: conservationism, environmental issues and green politics.

In *Crimson Stain*, the writer sets the tone from the very first poem, letting you know that the oppressors would stop at nothing, using any means necessary, for power or control...that it is up to us to use our own individual authority to stop them.

He touches upon the black and indigenous people...their struggles, whether against slurs, 'Rednekkks', the 'bible-belt', white hoods or the trauma of ropes dangling from trees. He touches upon the 'death god', '*who dances to the whims of his Puppeteer & the circle of tyrants from whence he came—*' questions the mercy of God for abandoning his children.

His poetry is diverse, and his images are sometimes very intimate and vivid. Yet he finds time for love. He refers to desire, as coming to him *'ghostly pale, resplendent in the finest black garments'*. He gives his *'slender, dark body as a gift.'*

'A Nubian vessel to hold,
Cradle, caress, stroke
From top to bottom,
Suckle like the sweetest fruit,
Adorn with kisses,
Strip bare,
Envelop in the folds of your slit.

The poet is weary of chasms in society, the faces of the 'haves', looking down upon, or scorning the everyday lifestyle of the 'have-nots'. In his description of them, the poet is poignantly touching: They are 'loathsome' of beauty, seeing it as darkness, because their eyes and hearts are warped. They cast judgements on those who do not seem to fit their own sense of values...a kind of stereotyping of the less fortunate.

He is picturesque with tender affections: *'a farewell kiss so damn good.'* Or *'a love that left you breathless',* and yet, despite temporary relief, the *'pain of loneliness lingers.'*

The Hole is one of the poet's most graphic and compelling pieces! In it he tells a tale of living in garbage worse than 'Third World squalor'', the fight for survival...

'Midnight trash runs & Dolomite flicks
Smoking spliffs & cherry incense
Skateboards & sloppy drunk couch sex
X-Box games & random stabbings.'

All this because of unscrupulous and callous landlords, who seemed to care only for themselves, the ails of poverty and an enslaved mentality. Amidst all this, the police is like an overseer, carrying out his master's bidding, in a zone where mass shootings and deceitful lies are commonplace. Yet there's hope and the poet show us how he was able to survive these atrocious conditions.

The call to justice, to awakening, rings through and through in Dee Allen's poetry, and his use of imagery and storytelling to highlight the dangers of the corporate few is vividly obvious at times. There's no call to a Christianity that did not serve him well, but an inner indomitable will to do the needful, to awaken brothers and sisters to the Light.

The poet gives voice to some of the exploited African countries: the Congo, Angola, Liberia, Sierra Leone...slowly being stripped of their gold and other natural resources. This is a very informative book and one which is enlightening and clarifying on the exploits of global capitalism, colonialism, and their methods.

4

These include tobacco, drugs, forest and animal industries, perversion of crops...exploitation of ancestral Africans and more. The poet is very vivid at times:

'So let our mother bleed
To fuel our machines
So let our mother bleed
For big company schemes

So let our mother bleed
So factories can pollute
Sky grows black from smoke
Because the bleeding's profuse.'

He calls for reparation, not apology, and sees a need to re-use this to re-build the forgotten ghettoes, where blacks are tugging at sunrise upon the dawns and sunsets on the horizons.

This book is a must read! Walk with the author as he takes you through the languishing raven, as she *'beats her black feathered wings.'* The class struggle or disparity between the poor and the privileged few, questioning the social justice for the indigenous, black people and other oppressed families.

The privileged are *'bred with the world's luxuries served to them on a silver platter'*, know nothing about the impoverished, about destitution and starvation, challenges for the poor, highlighted again and again in his very vivid poetry. The poet finally calls on our resilience and sacrifice, to stop all inhumane and repressive systems.

I believe firmly that you will enjoy *Crimson Stain* as I have. Sit back, brew your tea or coffee, and begin!

—**Manantita, a.k.a. The Lantern Carrier. Author, poet, RN, R**

CRIMSON STAIN
[2007]

LOYAL TO NONE

Choosing their weapons
Lust for prestige sets the pace
Choosing their methods
To keep you in a subservient place

The politicians
The law
The state
Loyal to none

The boss
Your job
Your pay
Loyal to none

Choosing their weapons
To ensure their hold on power
Choosing their methods
Whatever forces you to cower

The preacherman
The Bible
"Words of God"
Loyal to none

The police
Badge & gun
Excessive force
Loyal to none

Make your choice
And then make your stand
Just use your voice
So you're beholden to no man

Strike
Boycott
Direct action
Loyal to none

There is no authority
There is no authority but yourself*

W:2.21.07
[For Rez, Katrina & Ben Axiom.]
*This end-quote was originally written by English
Anarcho-Punk band Crass in 1983

Dee Allen.

ANXIOUS

Desire comes to me
Ghostly pale
Resplendent in the finest black garments
At some cabaret, early evening
Subdued lighting & gentler music
Getting to acknowledge
Her embrace
Her scent
Lips upon lips
Tasting some brown sugar
And won't come up for air
Slender fingers
Getting to recognise
The contours of her shape
Afraid of letting loose
Letting ardour be our guide—

We meet

Under closed, fluttering lids
Each night
Twisting & turning under blankets
This longing sustains me
And edginess unfolds
Simultaneously
Synthetic borders & geography
Keep us apart
Each night, you're in my thoughts
Longing for someone
I have yet to meet in the full flesh
Anxious to meet
Brown eye to green eye.

W: 2.23.07
[For Tracy Nunn.]

Dee Allen.

FRAGMENT 2007

Another society exists
In the shadows of this one
Recognising the beauty in something
As typically loathsome as darkness
When the sun blazes across the heavens
They are nothing but shunned or maligned
By their neighbours or blending
Into the everyday
Tedium, making like chameleons
Enduring the rigours of someone
Else's "rat-race"
As the sun descends & surrenders to the
Coming of dusk, they come out to play
Carpe Noctem
Seize the night
They drape themselves in dark
Attire of their choosing
Paint their faces in snow-white
Foundation, black, warm grey and
Sometimes red & pink, as this makes them
The most comfortable
They haunt the
Coffeeshops, in search of camaraderie,
Caffeine & poetry of romance &
Deepest emotions
They pour into clubs
To dance the whirly dance as
If this wretched world was going to
Come to an end tomorrow

Crimson Stain

They stand in dark corners of those
Clubs, preferring their own company over
Sharing it with fashion-fiends or
Casting judgement harsh upon those
Who don't fit the proclaimed
"Proper mould"—

W: 2.24.07

Dee Allen.

SEPPUKU*

Short flash of light
Explosive sound
No pain felt
In the throes of passion
A farewell kiss so damn good
It knocked you to the floor
A love that left you breathless
And still
The day grew colder by the minute
As red sap left you
Along with the encompassing loneliness
In the pitch black
There is relief
From the pain of living.

W: 3.16.07
[Inspired by the song "Crossroads" by Puerto Rican
Industrial musician Lady Mystery.]

*JAPANESE: "Suicide."

Crimson Stain

DEEP NORTH

Headed to the "promised land" in droves
Attracted to bright urban lights
Like a swarm of sepia-toned moths,
They arrive
In search of work,
Safer homes,
Altars to pray to,
In search of the peace that
Living in the so-called
"Bible Belt" did not give them.

What kind of god
Would allow its own children to
Endure the jail cell,
The slurs
Out of the mouths of babes & rednekkks,
The noose that broke the neck
From a tree
Strung-up
For the crime of
Being born Black,
The white hoods that made their Heaven
By making innocent lives Hell?
What kind of god
Would abandon its own children
To the mercy of hate?
To doors being shut to them
Because they are descendants of the enslaved?

Dee Allen.

They arrive
With a different kind of home in their hearts.
Amongst the dark mass, a young
Tsalagi* woman, her Black carpenter
Husband & their 2 daughters [one a half-breed]
Leave Virginia in the dust
Headed for the "promised land"
In the shadow of the Great Depression.

The Deep North welcomes them all.

W: 3.20.07
*What the Cherokee Indians call themselves.
Pronounced "Chah-lah-gee."

THE HOLE

This was Hell & home at the same time.

Rubbish
Covered the floor from front to back
A pisspoor substitute for carpet
Dirty dishes, piled, almost teetering over
In the kitchen sink
Recyclables
Barricade a formerly empty space
Behind the front door
Third World squalor
Was more glamourous than this—
Midnight trash runs & Dolemite flicks
Smoking spliffs & cherry incense
Skateboards & sloppy drunk couch sex
X-Box games & random stabbings
Mississippi Delta Blues & Hardcore Punk
Riotous sounds
Fight for attention & control over human ears—
Psychopathic old Peruvian landlord
Whore tried every trick in the proverbial
Book to remove us, but we stuck around &
Gotten under her wrinkled skin.

I went to college, kept myself clean,
protested the war, studied, belted out chants
in street demos, rolled with the Black Bloc
in such an environment.
A glimmer of order in a realm of chaos.

Dee Allen.

Under an ugly pink suburban home on
Westgate Avenue
Was a hole in the ground
Infamous throughout the San Francisco Bay Area
Underground Punk scene
Made possible by a thirtysomething Goth
And hella young Punks.

This was Hell & home at the same time.

W: 3.22.07
[For Cooper Quinton.]

CHAR

Grab the can of petrol straight off the ground
Douse the wooden steps
From one end to the next
Until they're moist to the touch
Pull the small box out of pocket
Strike a match against the dark strip
And let it drop
On the moist wooden steps
Watch it
Suddenly burst into instant flame
Conflagration stretching across
Until it consumes both sides
Dancing fire reduced wood to char
Crisp & black
Because it needed to be—

The damage is done
To the bridge
Connecting my life to that
Of a klepto, lover of pre-pubescent
Boys & the Nazi
Twisted cross.
Insane pale mistress of Saint Pete.

W: 3.27.07
[For Renée Fuentes a.k.a. Mistress Sydney Vicious.]

Dee Allen.

ARTWORK

Life is pain
Pain is life
Life's pain
She cannot endure alone
Overwhelming
She tries to cope
With the savage beating
Life has given her daily
Through creating art
In the privacy of her bedroom
She picks up a scalpel
And begins to carve
Skillful etchings
Shallow, but skillful
Neat, on a soft surface
Her latest piece brings
Tears to her eyes
Multiple etchings
A slice here, a slice there
Knife-made latticework
Cuts overlapping
On skin, arms & torso
Her tension is broken
Through creating
A scarred, sanguinary work of art.

W: 4.2.07

Crimson Stain

SOLDIER

There is another war
That the United States is involved in besides
The war on terrorism:
The war on freedom.
Freedom of the press
And this war has claimed its first captive
Behind enemy lines.
A soldier who fought a bloodless fight
To keep independent media from
Selfish corporate hands.

The lone soldier refused to give
The enemy the film they lusted after.
For standing ground in the face of intimidation,
The enemy answered back with internment.

For 226 days,
The soldier was held
Without committing a crime.
Iron bars stared him in the face.
Waning days passed by,
But internment couldn't break him down.
The enemy's weapons—
The grand jury, the courts—
Wouldn't take him down.
Outside of Dublin's concrete jailhouse walls,
Other soldiers have continued
The captive soldier's fight, armed with
Camcorders & documenting the ugly truth
As it happened

Dee Allen.

And he knows it.
Other soldiers demanded loudly
For his release, from outside of Dublin's walls &
beyond.

Then, one day, the captive soldier was free.
His war is not over.

W: 4.4.07
[For Josh Wolf.]

STRENGTH

Cannot be found or determined
Through an ancient "good book"
Or a minister's sermon

Nor drawn on bended knees
Through deep prayer
Nor could it be sought
In imaginary kingdoms in the air

But it lies in a real shrine
Where it pounds to exist
Inside the strongest muscle
The size of your fist.

W: 4.9.07

Dee Allen.

CRIMSON STAIN

Brighter than day, the sunlight reflects
Making each of them gleam
Individually & set into necklaces
Clear, beautiful stones in a storefront window.
The shine alone is enough
To bring you inside the store for a closer look.

The counter clerk eagerly
Shows you his vast collection of shiny stones
On display.
Only one of them catches your eye.
Pulling it from the display, you admire the
Prettiest stone from your fingertips.
Luminescent. Too beautiful for words.
One cannot help but wonder about its origins.

Where did it come from?
How did it get here?
What is it used for?

Deep in the heart of the Dark Continent,
Inside mineshafts, enshrouded in darkness.
With just a flashlight & tools,
Dirty hands extract stones from the earth
Against their will.
At the expense of their arms & legs.

From frontline massacres.
Gunfights between a ruthless state and
Its armed rebels.
Rain of bullets, instant rupture.

Fighting for possession of the mines.

Smuggled into nations nearby.
300,000 carats flood the world market each year,
At the behest of Western tastes.

For the glamour.
The look of social greatness,
All from a shining
Owning-class status symbol.
Epitome of wealth & prestige
In the First World.

For financing well-armed competition
Against the state

Supported by rival states. Rampant
Destruction of nature & society
In the Third World.

Angola
Liberia
Sierra Leone
Congo
Bostwana
Stripped to the bone

Of their precious resource.
Precious crimson spent
For precious gems
Deemed more valuable
Than human lives.

Dee Allen.

The jewel industry grows stronger,
As all colonial enterprises have over the centuries.

Now drop that stone.
It's stained
With the blood of Africans.

W: 4.14.07
[For Bakari Olatunji.]

BLACK MASQUE

Slip into black clothes
And most importantly, your masque
Before you lies
A most daunting task

Wars for conquest
Bioengineered crops
Spreading global Capitalism—
Here is where it stops

The streets are coloured
In a surge of black
On palaces of the rich
You wage the attack

Banks, shops, skyscrapers
All symbols of wealth
Generators of revenue
Attribute to this system's health

Smashed under the weight
Of rocks, kicks & blows
Whatever it takes to leave
Capitalism in death throes

The state responds—
Armoured police advance
To guard ruling class interests—
On with the swift, violent dance

Another battle on the avenue

Dee Allen.

Another steel fence torn
Amidst the gas & debris,
Another victory will be born

Because without you,
Social movements wouldn't persist
Without you,
There'd be no courage to resist.

W: 6.12.07
[For Danielle B. a.k.a. Sick Girl.]

Crimson Stain

PLEDGE

I vow
Not to eat the flesh of the
Animal kingdom's slain & not to
Wear their fur, feathers & wool.
They have suffered in the factory farms,
At the hands of man,
Too much in life.

I vow
Not to taste or inhale
Rolled tobacco which blackens lungs just as
Greed blackens a corporate executive's
Heart slowly.

I promise
Never to indulge in opiates
Which alters one's hold onto the real,
Elevates one from the depths of daily trials.
The higher you go,
The closer to oblivion you'll be.
Havoc wrought on body & mind.
Structural holocaust.
Face to face with the great black
Inevitable.

I will abstain
From liquid courage
Fluid solace
Bottled violence
80 proof homewrecker
Liver eater

Dee Allen.

Consume this & you'll fall over
Mental seducer
Equilibrium reducer
Blackout inducer
Nothing taints the blood quicker.

I will distance myself
From another substance
Dark as my disposition.
My cup will never again run over
With the liquids that
Cut into blissful slumber,
My nightly respite from this mortal coil,
Like an unsolidified dagger.
They shake incessant my nerves

If too much is ingested.

I make this pledge
So the remainder of my years here
Will yield a clean bill of health.
To show respect for brethren
That swim, fly & stalk the land
On four legs.
To keep the monsters—
Civilisation's poisons—
Away from my door.

Crimson Stain

One last thing:

I refuse to use the X as
My symbol, my chain of strength,
My talisman.
I want no connection to a
Plane of underground culture that
Forces the sober on everyone else.
Young militant vegan puritans.
Honestly, I can be STRAIGHT
WITHOUT claiming the EDGE.

W: 6.25.07

Dee Allen.

INVASIVE SPECIES

Quick ecology lesson:

A species of animal or plant
From one ecosystem will transport
Themselves to another, thereby
Introducing themselves to it.
Unto entering their new habitat,
The introduced species will crowd out
Native inhabitants, in a competition over
Available resources, usually land.
Soon after the introduced species will
Extend their reach into other areas
And repeat the process, which
Places native species at risk.
In addition, the number of invaders
Multiply over time;
Then they become a permanent part of the
ecosystem.

This lesson applies
To the inner city.

Invaders
From suburban tracts visit its
Concrete canyons, valleys of steel & glass,
Its avenues, its barrios,
Epicentres of non-White culture;
Then flood them with their amassing numbers.
The working and poverty classes are
Driven out, homes emptied.
Cityslaves & bulldozers do the rest.
Arising from out of nowhere,
Shining new boxy Bauhaus rendition buildings,
Affluence, soullessness & non-culture
Cover each street corner.
Monuments to smug, self-indulgent
Mock-European classiness.
The urban habitat is now a
City of the walking dead, for its true
Heart has already been impaled,
Exsanguinated the moment the
Invasive species gained their collective foothold.

Meanwhile, streets are cleaner, walkable,
Safer, as well-fed, well-dressed
Newcomers sip their wine, eat brie & wheat crackers,
Making themselves at home.

W: 6.15.07

Dee Allen.

EXSANGUINATION

From above, the metallic drill
Punctures & bores
Digging ever deeper
Until it reaches the core

And then suddenly,
It arose in a geyser
Blood from the body came
Higher & higher

Drenching the surface
Flowing through veins
There's no stopping it, it seems
Her body constantly drains

So let our mother bleed
To fuel our machines
So let our mother bleed
For big company schemes

So let our mother bleed
So factories can pollute
Sky grows black from smoke
Because the bleeding's profuse

So let our mother bleed
Out from her inner core
Her lifesblood continues to be
A motivation for pointless war

So let our mother bleed

Crimson Stain

So greedy bastards can have their niche
So let our mother bleed
And make their companies more rich

And our mother lies drained
Of all that she's worth
Society grew too dependent
Upon the blood of the earth.

W: 6.17.07

Dee Allen.

REFUSAL

For being transported to the New World by ship
From the Dark Continent's veldts
In chains & shackles,
For being reduced to a living
Commodity, sold at the auction block to the
Highest, wealthiest bidder,
For being compelled to work
Another man's property, whilst its owner
Was well-fed, comfortable,
For zero pay,
Long hours in the field & the big house,

For dividing whole families,
For debasing the role of a father in those
Families to ineffectuality,
For satisfying momentary sexual appetites
On females by force,
For capturing those that escaped to the North
On the words of another
Returned to the South
With their victimised brothers,
Harsh punishments await them there,
Leather lash scars bare back
Of a bound man many times over,
For erasing most traces of original language & culture
And shoving English words down many throats,
For convincing their "property" that
The Motherland was a figment of their imaginations,
For being denied freedom of movement
Unless it was on the plantation,
For being denied actual freedom itself,

For being reduced to the status of an insect—

For all of this,
The most you could say is:
"Sorry."
"Maybe an apology is in order."

This time around,
"SORRY" WON'T DO.
Neither "maybe" nor "an apology" will reverse
Over 400 years of crimes against humanity.
Crimes that were perfectly legal,
If you had wealth.
And the benefit of White skin privilege.
Offences that began with the Middle Passage.

Human rights violations that
Amnesty International never catalogued
During their own history.

The power structure you support had
Succeeded with my people what they had
Failed to do with American Indians on
Their own domain.

An apology is not what we need.
Pity isn't either. HELL NO.
We want the same thing that
The Nisei* & the Ashkenazim** received for
Surviving the inhumanities of
United States military enclosure &
German Fascist terror,
We want something that's past due.

Dee Allen.

WE WANT REPARATIONS. HERE. NOW.

Nothing but refusal
Will be shown for anything less.

We want compensation for perennial
Damage done to our people from the onset.
We didn't ask to come to your
Ancestor's colonies.
We didn't ask to be
Forcibly assimilated into the Anglo-Saxon
Protestant way of life.
We didn't clamour for torture & unpaid labour.

The ancient Radical Republican promise
Executive Field Order #15
Called for seizure of Southern plant
Aristocrats' plantations, set to be broken
Into divided land-plots, for the tenancy &
Ownership of former slaves.
"Forty acres & a mule"
Became another government lie.
A promise reneged upon.
Another in a litany of reasons why
Not to trust the State.
Or its representatives.
Self-described "servants of the people."

And—

What was that?

We've already gotten reparations?
In welfare benefits?

We're not asking for more crumbs.
That's what liberals want us to do.
Submit to the old master.

Extra crumbs will not
Push me or other Nubians above
The poverty line.
Formal, choreographed apologies,
Be they private or public,
Delivered by politician or scholar, will not
Enable us to rebuild our crumbling communities.

For
Four centuries of adverse treatment from a
Three-century old nation, I give my
Answer to your arrogance in just
Two words,
One finger,
Zero sympathy:

FUCK OFF.

W: 6.20.07
[For Queenandi & Marlon Crump.]

*American-born children of the first Japanese
immigrants in the United States.
**European Jews.

Dee Allen.

DERELICT
[SONG-LYRICS]

I am no one but I am
Known by everybody

Often seen by never heard
Just part of the scenery

Hated, ridiculed & shunned
For the way I live

I survive through every day
On what others give

Nothing to my name but a heavy load
And plenty of freedom

Never knowing where the road takes me
Where my next meal comes from

Left to the wolves in this cold world
Without a shred of sympathy

Underneath a bridge is shelter
Always open for vacancy

Humanity turned their back on me
These streets have no mercy
Less than human, how they treat me
Another night
In the life
Of a derelict

Crimson Stain

Humanity turned their back on me
These streets have no mercy
Just one in a million just like me
Another night
In the life
Of a derelict

W: 6.28.07
[Inspired by the music of Lycia & Tara Vanflower.]

Dee Allen.

OVERSEER

In his uniform of midnight black,
He storms into the urban landscape,
Seeking to right society's wrongs.
His regular stomping grounds:
The ghetto.
It is here that he goes to mete out his
Own brand of justice
On the poor.
Brandishing the ultimate equaliser,
All six chambers,
Locked & loaded, this self-proclaimed
Protector shoots first,
Asks no questions,
Lies about the incident later.
His black oak stick swings,
Batters skull & bone.
All for approval.
All for the dollars.
Inner sense of superiority, good as fed.
Repeated vulgar displays of power
Excused by the piece of silver he wears.

No different from the White Celtic
Overseer of yesteryear,
On horseback, toting shotgun & whip,
Hovering over scores of slaves
Working the cotton fields from
Sunrise to sundown.
One false move or none, it's
Whippings or death.
The overseer enforces the will of

Authorities greater than himself.

Who better to please the wishes of White masters
Than a cop, ready to betray
His own Black brethren?

W: 7.3.07

Dee Allen.

CAGES

Once upon a time,
On Friday the 13th,
Bad luck ran high.

Bad luck ran highest
For two ravens in flight,
On their way back to the nest.
Without warning,
Two nets ensnared
Two ravens, now seized by
Two powermad men and thrown into
Separate cages for
Display in their home.

Two ravens,
Once together,
Languishing apart
As their captors intended.

The next morning, one raven
Flew from his cage, left ajar,
Off to warn the flock about their
Captured sister & protect the nest.

The other raven remained inside her
Locked cage & remembers the
Bad fortune befallen on her & her mate.
She instantly recalled the wrong done to
Them both & sought to correct it

In escape.

With long beak and
Longer memory, the raven was determined to
Pick at the cage-latch, slowly and surely.
Once the cage was open, the raven
Beat her black feathered wings,
Quick flight towards freedom.

For her & her mate.

W: 7.15.07
[For Kim Rohrbach.]

Dee Allen.

CLASS WARFARE

There's no peace between classes.
Only war.

That war may have begun several centuries ago,
But the latest battle began the moment
Certain words fell from certain lips of
Sons & daughters of privilege—

The line was drawn between factions
Before any shots were fired
Created distance through actions
Cooperation had expired—

Refuse to share living space under one roof
Disrespecting the elders
Indigenous to this land
Disrespecting the POOR—
No solidarity
Just toxic air
Separated from the community
In the basement, unfair
Security guards, tall gates
Disturbing & vast
Restricting my movement
Unless I have a pass
Where's the equality?
Where's the social justice?
They are non-existent
In this "progressive" artifice
Sharing skills & resources?
They refuse

Crimson Stain

Even here, the indigent lose
Due to states of abuse

Became enemies when we should've been allies.

I was prepared to fight the good fight
Against a common adversary.
The concealed weapons of
Race & class privilege put an end to that.
In its place, a petty conflict
Without corpses or blood.

The ones who broke our trust:
Born with a silver spoon
Up their asses

Bred with the world's luxuries
Served to them on a silver patter
So they are free of stressing over
Starvation, thirst, destitution, want
And security.
Because they have been sheltered
Away from poverty, the
Privileged will never know the needs of the
Impoverished.
They will remain in darkness, despite their
Efforts to reach out to us, half-hearted.
Unless they toss their baggage aside.
Or kick it down.

Dedicated to saving an
Endangered woman's CHOICE in the U.S.A.
Whether or not to carry a growing seedling

Dee Allen.

Inside her 9 months long—

From the other side of the battlefield:

Pledged to making media
Untainted by corporate world influence
Through the lens of common people.
Honourbound to saving this world from
Cataclysms manmade through our stories.

Became enemies when we should've been allies.

They the privileged perpetrate
During activism on parade
Shouting: "WE ARE UNSTOPPABLE!
ANOTHER WORLD IS POSSIBLE!"

Another world will be impossible
To reach if oppressive systems
Still stand erect
In us & in movements.

Lessons learned in a battlefield
Called the United States Social Forum.

W: 7.25.07
[For Lola Bean.]

Crimson Stain

TWO

Condemned to walk the earth
And for naught
But survival for oneself
Or so I thought

Then I met my equal
Twisted into slender form
The sum of my desires
Shelter from any storm

Union of the lonely
Company of two
The world's vagaries never matter
When I'm with you

Partners-in-crime
Comrades-in-arms
Fallen prey
To each other's charms

What began as friendship
Like so many others
Ascends to the next level
Beneath the covers

The void is filled
The bed has shaken
Dormant secrets now revealed
In the passions awakened

Union of the lonely

Dee Allen.

Company of two
The world's vagaries shatter
When I'm with you

Partners-in-crime
Comrades-in-arms
Fallen prey
To each other's charms

The void is filled
The heart is mended
Together we walk a new path
Loneliness has ended.

W: 7.29.07 [For Kim Rohrbach.]

OFFERING

I am not a religious man,
But I want to make an offering.
Not to any alleged deity,
But to you.
As a token of devotion, I give to you my
Slender, dark body as a gift.
A Nubian vessel to hold,
Cradle, caress, stroke
From top to bottom,
Suckle like the sweetest fruit,
Adorn with kisses,
Strip bare,
Envelop in the folds of your slit,
Warm each other on the most brisk
Cold of evening,
Your skin against my own,
Show devotion without saying a word
Gyrations and sweat say it better—
Moans make the message clearer—
Our wills bend together.

Dee Allen.

I am not a wealthy man,
But I want to make an offering.
It has no monetary value, but it is a
Gift from me nonetheless.
I give my own body to you as a gift.
A Nubian vessel
Built for your pleasure & affection.
I am beholden to no one normally,
But I belong to you now.
Do with me what you will.

W: 7.30.07
[For Kim Rohrbach.]

TAPEWORM

When a person swallows the pork
That they've eaten, a little
Consequence grows.
In the shape of a larva.
Larva becomes tapeworm,
Attaches itself onto the intestines of its host.
What the host-body consumes, the tapeworm
Will consume.
It is a worm that doesn't slave away to get
What it wants as other organisms can.
That's what the host-body does.
No matter how much they eat,
No matter how hard they work,
The host-body never gets bigger.
But the tapeworm always does.
It expands to a size that matches
Its ravenous hunger.
Otherwise, it expires.

Dee Allen.

One other entity exists
With the self-same traits as the tapeworm.
It feeds & grows & expands
Off the hard work, time & energy of its
Living, struggling host.
Millions of bodies within one that are drained
By one greater parasite than a tapeworm:

CAPITALISM.

Both need hosts to live.
Both need to die.

W: 8.8.07
[Inspired by the speeches of Chairman Omali
Yeshitela from the Uhuru Movement.]

SOLDIER 2

"In sum, we are an army of dreamers and
therefore invincible."—Brad Will.

In the ongoing war
For the public's minds,
Another soldier leaves the safety of his bunker
And rushes straightaway into another
War-torn area.

Dangerously close to barricades,
Arms fire & explosions,
The lone soldier prowls through
Rubble-strewn cobblestone streets
With his weapon ready.
His mission: Shoot anything that moves.

Five enemy soldiers with the
Same plan, spot the lone soldier from afar.
His weapon's in plain sight.
The soldier's about to have
Unwanted company chase him.
As the five enemies close in on foot,
The lone soldier aims his weapon at
His pursuers. They aim their weapons at
The hunted one.

Two bullets
Stopped the lone soldier from completing his
mission.

Dee Allen.

Five enemy gunmen captured
On film & sent across the
World Wide Web in minutes.

The world mourns
For one lone casualty
In the propaganda war, armed only with his
Weapon-of-choice, a
Digital camcorder.
Into the heart of revolt went
A brave combatant from a vast army of dreamers.
Brave, but not so invincible.
Witness to a fiery struggle for autonomy
From corrupt statehood

Dead in Oaxaca one October. This soldier earned his
stripes.

W:8.13.07 [For Brad Will—1970-2006.]

Crimson Stain

SHINIGAMI*

The death god shows no mercy
And sows destruction,
As if his reign was threatened.
Summoned from the void,
Created in his maker's likeness,
The death god stands as an enemy to all life.

The death god laid nature to waste;
Opened the forests for further clearing,
Left the skies polluted with noxious gases,
Opened the path for global warming,
Let the corporations & science-monks
Tamper with plants, genetic twistings
Unfit to eat.
The death god brought 2 towers down;
Encouraged his subjects to seek revenge,
Wage the widespread bloodhunt for
All Allah's children.
Kill our freedoms in cold blood.
Fascism slowly rises as the new
Straightforward reality.
The death god brought on
Trials in secret, no judge,
No barrister, no jury,
Orgies of torture the world cannot see.
The death god sent youth into
Fields of warfare, deceased bodies
Continue to stack up in the desert
On both sides, military & civilian.
The death god wants the blood of youth
To spill for the blood of the earth.

Dee Allen.

The death god forces
Migrants & refugees from other lands to
Perish in oppressive heat before reaching
Their newest home.
Rifles are trained on those who survive.
The border is fortified threefold.
The death god abandoned millions of the poor
To rising stormwater, corpses afloat.
Armed occupiers
Have their city on lockdown.
The death god presided over scores of
Executions of transgressors,
Thin the coloured herd.
Empty the jail cells of Black & Brown,
Population reduction ordered from above.

The death god will fill the prisons
With any that oppose him.
He has weapons of mass destruction
To prove it. Do not tempt fate.
The death god has loyal servants on his side.
The wealthy are so much stronger
Because of their chosen deity. World eater.
The death god is pissdrunk
On excessive power.

The death god has evil thoughts
Planted into his hollow head,
Carried on the breath of mortal threats
And speeches.
The death god moves

On many strings
Pulled by another
Powerful, more malicious death god.
Man-made death god
Suspended from miniature strands,
Dances to the whims of his
Puppeteer & the circle of tyrants
From whence he came—

W: 8.14.07

*JAPANESE: "Death god."

Dee Allen.

WHITE TREE

Reclining under the shade of a tree.
A tree considered "forbidden space"—

White boys
Black boys
Co-existence
Destroyed
Malice
Dominates
Social fabric
Of Southern states
Allure of hate
No escape
State official
Threatens fate
On one kind
For dissent
For replying
In their own defence
To a stone hotel
Six were sent
The law points fingers
Murder, the charge
Malice lingers
Still at large

Reclining under the shade of a tree.
An area not to be crossed.
One day, just another outgrowth of nature.
The next day, mysterious long growths
Appeared. Three of them. Hung low.
Each ready to receive a fresh, dark neck—

W: 9.14.07

Dee Allen.

WATCH

These streets are watching
You with many eyes.

These streets are watching
You from lightposts above intersections
Of traffic, in the "worst" parts of any
Given metropolis.
Squadcars turn each corner,
Anticipating someone's false move,
A potential arrest.

These streets are secure now
With many electric eyes and extra cops.
The repressive flavour is almost
Commonplace enough to be part of the ecology.

Everyone is a suspect.
Criminals in the making.

Is the crime gone?
Are the drugs gone?
Are the gangs locked away?
Are we safer yet?

These streets are probing
Your intimate moments.
That couple kissing in the plaza has a
Closed-circuit captive audience.

The all-seeing eye of the state
Can watch your every move, wherever you go, at any

Given moment.
But its main gatekeeper
Has a massive pile of skeletal matter
In his closet.
A closet that just overflowed,
Bones and all—

W: 9.15.07

Dee Allen.

POISONBOX

Fingertips grip a
Small, slender box, aimed at
Another box you've become all too familiar with.
One touch of a key opens a veritable
Pandora's box.
Once activated, the box unleashes
Demons, desires, maladies, luxuries,
Simple distortions of the real
In living colour
For your entertainment & comfort.
You laugh, you smile, you cry, you groan, you
Salivate at all it presents.
All thought shuts down.
Capacity for reason all twisted up
Under the influence of facing countless
Flickering images—

Just sit back, relax, indulge
And go docile.
Let the poisons of this box flood your senses.

W: 9.15.07

DIVIDED HOUSE

United we fall
Divided we stand
Do unto others
And steal from your fellow man

United we fall
Divided we stand
Abuse thy neighbour
Is the rule of this land

Land of the greed
Home of the depraved
Freedom isn't free—
The reason most are [wage] slaves

We walk by faith,
Not by sight—
Faith in the dollar & flag,
The causes of mental blight

By his stars & stripes
We are healed—
But within the fabric,
Resentment reveals

To this republic
For which it stands—
Stocks & bonds for the wealthy
And crimes for the broke man

Privileged versus underprivileged

Dee Allen.

Rich versus poor
In God we trust—
And deepening class war

We the people
Form a perfect dis-union
Life under "free enterprise"
At its logical conclusion.

W: 10.07
[Inspired by a poem by Kim Rohrbach.]

Crimson Stain

NON-ENEMY

The man who prays to the East
Is not my enemy.
Neither is the person
Who wears a cloth upon
Their head or face out of tradition.
Neither are those who arrive here
From arid desert lands.
The family that attends
Mosques & worship Muhammhad & Allah are
No more a threat to me than
The middle-aged shopkeeper whose
First language is Farsi.
The Palestinians & Afghans do not terrorise
My neighbourhood and the
Lebanese do not make the streets on my block
Unsafe to walk through at night.
The Egyptians do not occupy my home or any
American's homes with their
Presence, uniforms, weapons & neo-colonialist law.
Critical thinking is under attack at
Higher learning institutions besides mine and
It's not the Syrians who are kicking out
Instructors one by one.
The Iraqi people
Aren't deserving of my detestation & rage.
One Fallujah*
Is not enough.
All of the Middle East's progeny did not
Make war with me or grab the land beneath my feet
Or called the petrol within it theirs.
The Middle Easterners & Muslims did not

Dee Allen.

Stage outright bombings, shootings and jailhouse
Torture on me in my town.

But that's what
The United States has done to them.
Again & again.

The real Fascism is homegrown.

W: 10.25.07
[In response to "Islamo-Fascism Awareness Week".]

*A city in Al-Abnar province of Iraq, where an anti-
colonial rebellion took place against the U.S. military
curfew over the area. On March 31, 2004, after U.S.
troops opened fire on Iraqi civilians at a closed-down
school 3 days earlier [resulting in 17 dead and 70
wounded], Iraqi rebels fought back by attacking a
convoy
and dragging & burning 4 American military
contractors from Blackwater.

Crimson Stain

WISTFUL

Sad, but not tearful.
Down, but not suicidal.
The general feeling I'm
Overcome with today.
Immersed in thought,
Uncertain of the days to come.
The warmth of bygone days
Is disappearing.
It is during this time that
An old man approaches.
As he passes through, the ancient one
Brings gentle bumps on my skin,
Penetrates my very bones with the icy chill
He leaves behind.
Steady downpours are sure to follow
This aged stranger's passage when
Everything is already dead.
Leaves on trees,
A memory now, tailor-made for postcards.
As that old man continues to saunter by
Deliberate & slow,
I fear the future,
My future,
And it doesn't look bright.
Sad, but not tearful.
Down, but not suicidal.
Just downright wistful.

W: Day Of The Dead 2007

Dee Allen.

MOLOTOV

1 part cloth.
3 parts petrol.
Hell under glass.

Pick a bottle, any bottle
And fill it with
Flammable content.
Stick in the rag,
With one half in the fluid,
One half protruding.
Set the protruding rag ablaze

And throw it at those
Who threaten your life.

When there's civil unrest
And the state's agents move in to
Trap you in the streets,
Don't play victim.
Play barsita.
Serve them a hot bottle of trouble.
Turn your darkest hour into cocktail hour.

W: Guy Fawkes Day 2007
[For Crudo, Nagi & Serge.]

SLUMBER

Riding the rails again
Beneath the city of Saint Francis.
I climb aboard another train
Fatigued from head to toe.
The globe's weight bearing down on my skull,
Legs in constant motion, crave rest now.
Both eyes scan the train for any
Available seat.
Front. Back. Last car. Next car.
Found.
No reading, no patience for the
Near pitch black outside my window, I'm
Down in the seat.
Tunnel riding.
Eyelids heavy,
Awaiting sleep.
Now the lids shut out
The train, its passengers & the world's cares.
One-way voyage to relaxation.
Final destination: Bliss

As
my
body
lies
so
still—

W: 11.10.07
REV: 1.2.23

Dee Allen.

CRIMSON DROPS
[2012-2022]

REAWAKENING

In the season
  Of bare skeletal trees
    And freezing, frequent rain,
      Something long assumed
        Dead reawakened
          Among nature's
            Dead things—

                    A quiet library
                  With rows of desks,
                  With rows of pensive
                Students, hunched over
              Notebooks & textbooks, pen in motion
            Over one, data transfer
          From the other, silent synchronicity
        And me putting my own
      Intellectual capital to work—Powerful Birmingham
    Alabama jailhouse essay
      From Martin Luther King in my
        English textbook
          Fight for equal treatment
        Black civil rights in a racist society
                  Catalyst
            Fuel
          For cerebral
                    Engine stirring back
                      Into operation after
                        Seven long years
                          Of inertia
                            Lack of productivity
                              Creative

A most frightening prospect
  For all sensitive
    & literary—

Crimson Stain

Machinery
 Under the cranial hood
   Turns & turns
      Faster it churns
         Processing of fuel
            Acquired with both
               Eyes & ears
                  Within seconds
                     Like any well-tuned machine
                     Creativity
                        Once started up
                           Lets itself be heard
                           Loud
                              Aggressive
                                 Demanding
                                    Like an old English
                                    Hardcore Punk song from the 80s
                                    "4 Minutes Past Midnight"
                                       By Antisect
                                       Urgently

                              BUST

                     Out of the speakers
                     From the opening
                        Few notes—

In the season
   Of bare skeletal trees
      And freezing, frequent rain
         That
            Something long assumed
               Dead

Dee Allen.

My ability
To write

Reawakened

I have a purpose
Again
Besides college drone.

W: 6.4.12

REFUGE

There is a city
Inside my chest
Built from

Life-long love
For the Underground.

Buried beneath my chest,
The great city stands
Populated with
Asylum seekers,
Genuine tribes of the night.
Goths, Rivetheads, Steampunks,
Punks, Metalheads, Rastas, Hip Hop Heads
Find refuge from
The destructive
Mainstream and
Their heinous values.
My inner self,
Drifting between the tribes
That call him "brother",
Lives there for the same reason.

On every other block,
There are ballrooms
Booming with sounds
From the Underground.
Their walls vibrate with
Darkwave, EBM*, Steampunk, Trip Hop,
Hardcore Punk, Heavy Metal, Reggae, Hip Hop,
Their floors shake with

Dancing, partying and
Occasional skate-ramps.
Carnival side-shows with
Risky human tricks
Jim Rose style
A common occurrence.
Tattoos, piercings, henna, Manic Panic©
Coloured hair, lavish costumes, goggles, stilts,
Dreadlocks, yarn falls, chain mail, boots
In assorted styles,
Fire-dancing
Fit the garish
Urban scenery.
Overnight,
The great city
In my heart
Felt more
Emptier.
The night tribes
Have disappeared.
The street carnivals
Have stopped.
The booming ballrooms
Went silent.
Dancing, partying,
Skateboarding shows,
Stilt walking,
Fire performance,
Actions of yesterday.
Every block,
Desert bare.
My inner self,
Sole occupant left

In the great subcultural
Ghost town.

But he'll manage.
A lone wolf
Always acts
Independently anyway,
Knows his terrain,
Lives off it
And that makes
Him and me
Feel no less
Lonesome.

W: Chinese New Year 2018

*Electronic Body Music. Another name for
"Industrial music".

THE PIG'S YEAR

One new
Poetry book
The fourth
Magazine-sized
Front cover shows
The aftermath of
Destruction by fire
Scorched bare skeleton
Deep East Oakland
Commercial building
Everything it held
Rests in soot,
Another piece of me
Printed in a thick
New school textbook
For all ages, for
All poverty scholars
And their supporters owning
Race, class, education
Privilege,
Book promotion
Travels to L.A., Florida, Tennessee,
Who knows where else,
A few more
Pieces of me
Spread out between
Four new anthologies
The experiences and feelings
Of other writers enclosed
Within bound pages—

So far, for me,
This new year—
The pig's year
To the Chinese—
Isn't laced with
A single
Catastrophe—

W: 2.26.19
[For Sue Ellen Pector.]

SCARLET TRIANGLE

Desperate bid
For re-election
Social media master plan:
Twist public perception

Of who the real
Public enemy is
The real dangerous mob
The real security risk

"And you shall know them
By this distinctive sign":
Scarlet triangle
Inverted design

Bright red as anger
Hardly concealed
Bright red as blood wrath
On these streets so real

Resurrected old
Nazi death camp symbol
Mark for political foes—
Divisive, un-civil

Yet Antifa, the so-called threat
Fights for community
Fights for all races
Fights for unity

Crimson Stain

Smear campaign by advert
From a national security angle—
Only Fascists would dare
Use a scarlet triangle.

SURVIVAL INSTINCT

Why these choices?

Because of desperation.
Everybody wants somebody to save them from Hell,
Right?

Because of subsistence.
Everybody needs to eat and drink,
Right?

Because of self-medication.
Everybody wants to numb their lifeache,
Right?

Because of levels of endurance.
Everybody needs a home, mounds of trash or not,
Right?

Because of this profane existence.
Everybody wants to climb out of poverty,
Right?

Because of instinct.
Nobody wants to stay at the bottom,
Right?

One must do what
One must to keep on surviving, even in Hell,
Right?

W: Passover 2021
[In response to an untitled poem by The Unrated
Poet from Kenya.]

WARSTORM*
[SONG-LYRICS]

Everything we have
Everything we know
Turns into dust
In a single blow

Everything we see
Everything is bright
Right before the boom
Incinerates us from sight

After the bombs
After the nuclear fire
Ashen product of the warstorm
Birthed from dominance, political ire

W: 1.30.22

*To be performed with 4 or 5 drums and vocals done
on a bullhorn. Full, tribal sound.

THINGS FALL APART

Things fall apart
In times of war,
In loss of regularly
Scheduled lives and more.
Comfortable homes,
Farms and markets
Singled out by unexpected
Missiles—convenient targets.
These times of war
Only tyrants crave
Flattened cities, submission,
Every person, their slave.
But the Ukrainian survivors
Will rise above the gloom
To arrive at a brighter future
Where flowers still bloom.

W: 3.13.22
[For Stephanie Larkin.]

CARRION
[SONG-LYRICS]

Anger
Favourite deadly sin for you
Levelled
At the successful of different, darker hue

Just what the people want—
Another authoritarian
You're good for nothing—
Except fresh carrion

CHORUS 1: Go

        Drop dead!
        The ravens will eat well! [TWICE]

        Tearing meat from bone with their beaks
        You would make a splendid feast

        So

        Drop dead!
        The ravens will eat well!

Wrath
At the intelligent sister bound to prosper
Your picture on my screen doesn't lie—
Mass media racist fucker

This green earth's too good for you
To get buried in
You'll serve black winged animals best
As fresh carrion

Crimson Stain

90

CHORUS 2: Go

Drop dead!
The ravens will eat well! [TWICE]

Use their beaks, pluck out your eyes
Fitting end for the felcher I despise

So

Drop dead!
The ravens will eat well!

W: 3.19.22 [For Tucker Carlson.]

THEOTOXIN
[SONG-LYRICS]

Following my own desires
Fills you with dismay
A misled sinner in your eyes
You show me "a better way"

"Your life will improve if you
Let the good lord inside"
Catalyst for all repression
From censorship to genocide

CHORUS: Your almighty god is poison
            To my heart and mind
            Would kill my individuality
            And render me blind

Losing my freedom
In the shine of heavenly light
Onward, commence to stumble
Walking by faith, not by sight

You won't be satisfied until
This planet becomes a theocracy
The saintly life you offer means
Subservience to a greedy preacher's fantasy

Crimson Stain

[REPEAT CHORUS]

Biblical scriptures
Meaningless noise
Keep your fucking poison
From me! That's your choice!

THE CURSIVE WRITER

What moves me forward
Are words of encouragement
From a 75-year old
Bed-bound friend with half of his body
Frozen in paralysis from a sudden stroke:

"NO! DON'T GIVE UP!"

His reply
To my lamenting
Living through
Writer's block for 3 weeks, aired
Thoughts of hanging up

Creative writing, Spoken Word.

Though barely conscious
In his Castro* hospice
Bed, he must've known
Immediately without
The two things that made me <u>me</u>,

Creative writing, Spoken Word,

I would be
Another man
Following someone's goddamn
Conform-to-comfortable illusions programme.

Another voice silenced.

Couldn't be that if I tried.

Conventions
Were meant to be challenged.
Authorities
Were meant to be defied.
Nobody knew these notions & actions

Better than The Cursive Writer.

Born in White Conservative Fort Recovery, Ohio,
Raised some of the time in Florida,
Religious repression, racism observed & met in both
places,
Drafted into the Navy for a brutal, unpopular war in
Vietnam

That compelled him to defect

To the side of peace.

San Francisco,
City of 48 hills, 49 miles,
Facing the Bay & the Pacific,
Boasting hot autumns & foggy summers,
Nerve centre for the flower power counterculture

Became his home, in spirit & fact,

Even during these pestilent days,
This ongoing colonial project,
This stolen indigenous continent,
This lone, chest-beating, macho superpower,

The United States of America

Had nothing he, lover of nature & tribes, wanted.

The Christians'
Sky God
Was not his.

Black Robes'
Colonising gospel
Was not his.

White Robes'
Night-riding terror
Was not his.

The Forever Wars
For dominance
Were not his.

American Killers'
Ghost-making ways
Were not his.

Gringo's
Pale-skin privilege & entitlement
Were not his.

Policeman's Credo
"Move along! Nothing to see here!"
Was good as ignored.

Crimson Stain

The Empire USA**
And its machinations
Were never his.

Old school iconoclast,
Comrade of 14 years
Preferred

The Rolling Stones over The Beatles,
Miles Davis over Chet Baker,
Tall boy bottled water over tall boy canned beer,
Salma Hayek over any White lady celeb,
Pristine ecology over polluted ecology,
Hazelnut milk over cow's milk,
Togetherness over separation that currently exists—

He had found
Home and
Acceptance amidst

Other war veterans,
Native Americans,
Musicians,
Activists,
Artists, misfits
And last,
But never least,
Poets.

You know,
The people USA
Finds disposable

Unless they can master
Information
Technology
And the art of redeveloping
Certain city neighbourhoods
With a presence
More homogenised
Than cow's milk.

Hospital work
Occupied his time
And his pockets kept
Filled with ducats.

Since retirement,
My fellow
Herbivore,
Vegetarian-turned-vegan,

My fellow poet
Would be found
In Sacred Grounds
Or Café International,

The elderly white-bearded man
In the black fedora hat
With 3 feathers, Hopi-style jacket with pins,
Shiny coloured button-down shirt,
Metal rings decorated
Eight of his 10 fingers

Crimson Stain

Typing out
His next opus,
Mosaic of words,
Grist for the next open mic performance
On his silver Apple laptop computer,

Technological reading
Aid before a live mic,
Backed up
By musical legends:

Greer Rockett on trumpet,
Luis Romero on bongos,
David Erdreich on sax—
Jazz/poetry/activism synthesis—

The Beatniks
Of yesteryear would've yelled
"WILD, DADDY-O!", "GO, MAN, GO!",
Would've rallied behind

Him, The Cursive Writer.

Sunset years
Found him acquiring amazing
Literary & oratory gifts, rich with wit & wisdom.

Native American medicine bringer
In White skin. His medicine was his
Words, to keep us on the right side of history.

He always went
To where naked
Injustice shown itself—wrong side of history—

Our ethical convictions,
His and mine,
Run along parallel lines.

He was also
The biggest fan
Of my written work

And one of the extreme few
This old misfit would call
"Friend"

But this long rambling poem ain't about me.

It's about the man,
My poetry brother,
Who knew the importance of
Having one's own voice
And its use for good,
Handed out one piece of advice
Whilst barely conscious, bed-bound on
The last time we met:

Crimson Stain

"NO! DON'T GIVE UP!"

I haven't. The rollerpoint pen
In my hand still moves over paper
Because of you, Richard.

W: 5.22 to 7.22
[For Richard Sanderell, The Cursive Writer—1946-
2021.]

*A historically Queer neighbourhood in San
Francisco. Formerly Eureka Valley.
**Pronounced: "Oo-sah." Sanderell's way of saying
"U.S.A."

DILEMMA, DILEMMA
[MICRO-FICTION]

Seven doors. Seven choices. Dilemma, dilemma. Facing these doors in this surreal corridor taunts me with my ability to decide.

What could be behind them? Six are dove-white, one is canary-yellow. Facing them also fills me with trepidation and self-doubt.

What if the yellow door leads to paradise or a prize?

What if the other door leads to perdition, Elysian Fields in flames, and the other 6 doors have prizes?

What holds me captive? Fear, making the wrong choice. But I'll never know the outcome unless I try to break free from fear's spell and step forward to turn the knob—

W: 5.24.22
[For Alison Schoew.]

SHED NO TEARS
[SONG-LYRICS]

The ghetto
Is a sad place
Where ten someones passed away

Flight of lead
Pierced Black skin
Gunman's ill will—fear of being "replaced"

Productive lives
Needlessly cancelled
Consign to eternal rest

Ten someones
Taken from their families
By a stranger everyone grew to detest

He thought the armour
Under his combat fatigues
Would protect him from fired retaliation

Heavy hearts, flower bouquets
For souls taken in hate
We show compassion, the other condemnation

CHORUS: Shed no tears [3 TIMES]
         For the man without honour

         Shed no tears [3 TIMES]
         For the murdering fucker

[REPEAT CHORUS]

W: Memorial Day 2022
[Requiem for the Buffalo 10.]

ARACHNID

She's not hardwired for predation.
Mating, then killing
Just ain't her thing.
Her instinct is more creative.

Red and black roaming spider,
A black widow, mind you,
Crawls from one open mic to the next,
Endowed with gifts for storytelling & rhyme:

Seduction of Count Dracula,
Alienation felt like Frankenstein,
Merlin's gift for magic,
Red Riding Hood's lustful curiosity about the wolf,

Pitch-perfect
Lava flow of feelings needed to be released,
Spoke of vulnerability, surviving hard trials, heart's
Transition from pain to strength.

Tennessee arachnid,
Widow in red,
Latina Goth
Prodigal Poet

Spins her web,
Catches many flies
Using the best
Possible words on hand.

W: Marilyn Monroe Birthday 2022
[For Gina Carillo a.k.a. Black Widow.]

REGRESSION

Gimme an S
Gimme a U
Gimme a P
Gimme an R
Gimme an E
Gimme an M
Gimme an E

Gimme a C
Gimme an O
Gimme a U
Gimme an R
Gimme a T!

What's that spell?

Well,

America's still
The land of freedom.
Provided that
Men in jet black robes behind pulpits,

Who will never
Experience the pain
Of childbirth, in bringing a fresh
New human into our world, propagate our species,

Can control
Women's bodies
With reams of laws

Crimson Stain

And outlawed clinics

Closed for business.
The urban
Back alleys
Are about to get some.

Theocratic
Regression
To "the good old days"
That never were—

America's experiencing a rebirth.

Order of the day:

Denial of personal choice.
Contained bodily autonomy.
Breed on demand.

Thank the judges, ladies.

They gifted
You Hell.
Give them the same. And stronger.
Your womb, your choice, both at stake.

W: 6.28.22

FLAMETHROWER

My internal spirit of rebellion
Is far from calm—
Incendiary

Anger builds
Single spark ignites
Observing injustice

From figures of authority,
Power moves, prejudice—
Inferno in the making

Refusing to be
The next victim, the next pawn,
I know these sensations well—

Long ago, I marched on California's streets
Against animal torture,
Middle East oil wars,

Biotech,
White supremacy,
Police murder—

Inferno found release
Through the plastic weapon
Clutched in my ebony hands

Felt like
An assault rifle
And equally as loud.

Crimson Stain

My finger on the trigger,
My lips on the mic piece,
One breath and

The inferno spat forth. Forceful
Tongue of flame
Pure lyrical fire.

White-hot
Righteous rage
Aimed at the police line.

Heat searing
Through lawmen's egos

Catchy chant and hook:

*TÚ PUERCOS
PROTEGEN
A LOS RICOS!* *

Additional flames
Were unleashed
As names of the dead

Protectors of capital
Saw fit
To exterminate:

*AYANNA JONES!
ALAN BLUEFORD!
ERNESTO DUENEZ!*

Following my voice
Inching forward like their steps,
The march of people had added power.

There's no
Taking back
The truth.

The streetbound mass and the lawmen
That followed and fenced us
In front of the cop shop

Were left
Wondering who
I am.

I am
More than a single man
With a sonic flamethrower,

Battery-powered
Loudhailer**
In my tight ebony fist.

I am lyrics.
I am fire.
I am social justice.

W: 7.17.22
[For Maureen Medina, Laura Hawkins-Grevel and
Jenny Kalahar.]
*SPANISH: "You pigs protect the rich!"
**Australian word for "bullhorn".

PRINT APPEARANCES

*LOYAL TO NONE > POOR MAGAZINE
[online]: March 2007 and CAPITALISM ATE MY
PUPPY [' zine] #2: Spring 2008.

*SEPPUKU > OUT OF OUR [magazine]: Volume
5: January 2010.

*DEEP NORTH > POOR MAGAZINE: August
15, 2007 and STREET SHEET [newspaper]
[BLACK HISTORY & FUTURES MONTH ISSUE
]: February 2023.

*SOLDIER > STREET SPIRIT [newspaper]: June
2008.

*STRENGTH > OUT OF OUR Volume 3: July
2009.

*BLACK MASQUE > MODESTO ANARCHO
['zine] #6: Winter 2008.

*PLEDGE > TO THE RESTLESS ['zine] #2:
Summer 2008.

*INVASIVE SPECIES > POOR MAGAZINE: July
2, 2008 and STREET SPIRIT: June 2008.

*EXSANGUINATION > STREET SPIRIT: June
2008.

*DERELICT > STREET SPIRIT: June 2008.

*OVERSEER > THE BURNING SPEAR
[newspaper]: November/December 2007.

*CLASS WARFARE > POOR MAGAZINE: August
7, 2007.

*WHITE TREE > FORUM [magazine]: Fall 2007
and 16TH & MISSION REVIEW [magazine] #4:
November/December 2007.

*WATCH > LIVING IN THE LAND OF THE
DEAD: AN ANTHOLOGY OF ANTHOLOGIES:
FAITHFUL FOOLS POETRY [2004-2014]:
Freedom Voices/Faithful Fools, 2017. [Consolidated
with
another poem & printed as "Untitled"—odd editorial
decision.]

*POISONBOX > 16TH & MISSION REVIEW #6:
March/April 2008.

*DIVIDED HOUSE > VEGANARCHY ['zine]
#1: Summer 2009.

*NON-ENEMY > SYNCHRONIZED CHAOS [
webzine]: April 28, 2009 and SOMETHING
WORTH REVISING ['zine] #4: Summer 2017.

*MOLOTOV > MODESTO ANARCHO ['zine]
#6: Winter 2008.

*WISTFUL > MONTEREY POETRY REVIEW [magazine]: Spring 2023.

*SCARLET TRIANGLE > WRITE OUT LOUD [blog]: October 19, 2020.

*CRIMSON STAIN > POETS 11: 2014 [anthology]: San Francisco Public Library/Friends Of The San Francisco Public Library, 2015.

*WARSTORM > PEACE AGAINST WAR [anthology]: edited by Maid Corbić, 2022.

*THINGS FALL APART > HOPE [anthology]: Qantara House Books, 2022, THE COMPASS [webzine] #5: June 2023 and A THIN SLICE OF ANXIETY [webzine]: June 29, 2023.

*THEOTOXIN > THE OFFSHOOT [webzine]: April 2022 and POETRY EXPRESS NEWSLETTER: May 2022.

*DILEMMA. DILEMMA > FREEDOM: WRITTEN TALES CHAPBOOK #3 [anthology]: Written Tales, 2022.

*SHED NO TEARS > HERON CLAN [magazine] #10: April 2023.

*ARACHNID > THE ANTONYM [webzine]: July 17, 2022.

*REGRESSION > <u>BENICIA HERALD</u> [newspaper]: Wednesday August 3, 2022. [Included in the
column *Going The Distance #101.*]

*FLAMETHROWER > <u>LAST STANZA</u> [magazine] #10: Fall 2022.

About the Author
Dee Allen.

African-Italian performance poet based in Oakland, California. Active on creative writing & Spoken Word since the early 1990s. Author of 7 books—*Boneyard, Unwritten Law, Stormwater, Skeletal Black* [all from POOR Press], *Elohi Unitsi* [Conviction 2 Change Publishing], *Rusty Gallows: Passages Against Hate* [Vagabond Books] and *Plans* [Nomadic Press]— and 70 anthology appearances under his figurative belt so far. *Crimson Stain* is Allen's 8th book to date.

About EYEPUBLISHEWE

Eye Publish Ewe is a brand new publishing company, founded in San Francisco. Art, music, video, poetry, and other literature will find inclusive shelter here. Quality work produced by the artists' hearts, minds, and souls rather than commercial interests will have this as a home. All are welcomed with open minds and hearts and eyes to the future. Together we will publish art for humanity's sake.

EPE Titles

Where Grasses Bend: Poems from Portland to Steens Mountain in the Time of Plagues by **Mimi German** ISBN: 979-8-9870259-5-6

The Green Notebook: Poems on Family, Relationships, Spirituality, Self-Enquiry, Recovery, ACA, Disruption, Death, Walking Through the Mirror, and Cats by **John Angell Grant** ISBN: 979-8-98702589-6-3

Morning Tanka: A journal of thank you notes between lovers, California poems in the style of traditional Japanese form poetry In English and Japanese by **Merecedes Dugger** and **Dane Ince** translations by Yuri Miki ISBN: 979-8-9898764-0-2

EPE Titles Coming Soon

A House without Walls: Existential Journeys and Love Poems to Mexico by **Lesley Constable**

La Naturaleza del Amor: Poems in Spanish and English by **Martin Del Toro Gutierrez**

www.ingramcontent.com/pod-product-compliance
Lightning Source LLC
Chambersburg PA
CBHW030313130626
46549CB00002B/835